Desk Calendar
© 1994 Antioch Publishing Company
Edited by Jill Wolf

Inquiries about the artist
may be directed to:

The Kiki Collection
500 North Robert Street
Studio 302
Saint Paul, Minnesota 55101
1-800-945-5454

Published by
Antioch Publishing Company
Yellow Springs, Ohio 45387
ISBN 0-7824-4742-2
Printed in the U.S.A.

Cover Painting:
Many Strong and Beautiful Women

Sweet Secrets

MANY STRONG AND BEAUTIFUL WOMEN

UNDATED ENGAGEMENT CALENDAR

Featuring the artwork of
Kiki Oberstenfeld de Suarez

Kiki

Antioch Publishing Company ✳ Yellow Springs, Ohio

January

1 _____

2 _____

3 _____

4 _____

5 _____

6 _____

January

7

10

8

11

9

12

January

13 ——————————

16 ——————————

14 ——————————

17 ——————————

15 ——————————

18 ——————————

Friendship with one-self is all-important because without it one cannot be friends with anyone else in the world.

– Eleanor Roosevelt

I Love Myself Very Much

January

19 ——————————————

20 ——————————————

21 ——————————————

22 ——————————————

23 ——————————————

24 ——————————————

January

25

26

27

28

29

30

January * February

31

1

2

3

4

5

The only thing to do
is to hug one's friends
tight and do one's job.

— Edith Wharton

The Embrace

February

6 ⎯⎯⎯⎯⎯⎯⎯⎯⎯⎯⎯⎯⎯⎯⎯⎯⎯⎯

9 ⎯⎯⎯⎯⎯⎯⎯⎯⎯⎯⎯⎯⎯⎯⎯⎯⎯⎯

7 ⎯⎯⎯⎯⎯⎯⎯⎯⎯⎯⎯⎯⎯⎯⎯⎯⎯⎯

10 ⎯⎯⎯⎯⎯⎯⎯⎯⎯⎯⎯⎯⎯⎯⎯⎯⎯

8 ⎯⎯⎯⎯⎯⎯⎯⎯⎯⎯⎯⎯⎯⎯⎯⎯⎯⎯

11 ⎯⎯⎯⎯⎯⎯⎯⎯⎯⎯⎯⎯⎯⎯⎯⎯⎯

February

12

13

14

15

16

17

February

18 ——————————

19 ——————————

20 ——————————

21 ——————————

22 ——————————

23 ——————————

Spiritual power can
be seen in a person's
reverence for life —
hers and all others,
including animals
and nature . . .

— Virginia Satir

**The Moon Doesn't
Know Where to Go!**

February

24 ———————————

25 ———————————

26 ———————————

27 ———————————

28 ———————————

29 ———————————

March

1

2

3

4

5

6

March

7

10

8

11

9

12

March

13

14

15

16

17

18

March

19

22

20

23

21

24

March

25

26

27

28

29

30

For is it not true that human progress is but a mighty growing pattern woven together by the tenuous single threads united in a common effort?

— Soong Mei-ling (Madame Chiang Kai-shek)

The Miracle

March ∗ April

31

1

2

3

4

5

April

6

7

8

9

10

11

April

12

13

14

15

16

17

April

18 ————————————————

————————————————

————————————————

————————————————

————————————————

————————————————

————————————————

19 ————————————————

————————————————

————————————————

————————————————

————————————————

————————————————

————————————————

20 ————————————————

————————————————

————————————————

————————————————

————————————————

————————————————

————————————————

21 ————————————————

————————————————

————————————————

————————————————

————————————————

————————————————

————————————————

22 ————————————————

————————————————

————————————————

————————————————

————————————————

————————————————

————————————————

23 ————————————————

————————————————

————————————————

————————————————

————————————————

————————————————

————————————————

Women's work is always toward wholeness.

– May Sarton

Teachers Change the World

April

24

27

25

28

26

29

April ✶ May

30

1

2

3

4

5

May

6 ——————————————

7 ——————————————

8 ——————————————

9 ——————————————

10 ——————————————

11 ——————————————

Harmony exists in difference no less than in likeness, if only the same key-note govern both parts.

— Margaret Fuller

Building Bridges

May

12 ——————————————————

15 ——————————————————

13 ——————————————————

16 ——————————————————

14 ——————————————————

17 ——————————————————

May

8 ——————————

9 ——————————

0 ——————————

21 ——————————

22 ——————————

23 ——————————

May

24

25

26

27

28

29

We must have
perseverance and
above all confidence
in ourselves. We
must believe that
we are gifted for
something . . .

– Marie Curie

**Mommy, Help Me
Touch the Stars**

May ∗ June

30

2

31

3

1

4

June

5

8

6

9

7

10

June

11 ————————————

12 ————————————

13 ————————————

14 ————————————

15 ————————————

16 ————————————

Woman can best refind herself
by losing herself in some kind
of creative activity of her own.

    — Anne Morrow Lindbergh

Daydreams

June

17 ————————————————

20 ————————————————

18 ————————————————

21 ————————————————

19 ————————————————

22 ————————————————

June

23

24

25

26

27

28

June ⋆ July

29 ⎯⎯⎯⎯⎯⎯⎯⎯⎯⎯⎯⎯⎯⎯

2 ⎯⎯⎯⎯⎯⎯⎯⎯⎯⎯⎯⎯⎯⎯

30 ⎯⎯⎯⎯⎯⎯⎯⎯⎯⎯⎯⎯⎯⎯

3 ⎯⎯⎯⎯⎯⎯⎯⎯⎯⎯⎯⎯⎯⎯

1 ⎯⎯⎯⎯⎯⎯⎯⎯⎯⎯⎯⎯⎯⎯

4 ⎯⎯⎯⎯⎯⎯⎯⎯⎯⎯⎯⎯⎯⎯

July

5

8

6

9

7

10

July

11

14

12

15

13

16

July

17 ⎯⎯⎯⎯⎯⎯⎯⎯⎯⎯⎯⎯⎯⎯

20 ⎯⎯⎯⎯⎯⎯⎯⎯⎯⎯⎯⎯⎯⎯

18 ⎯⎯⎯⎯⎯⎯⎯⎯⎯⎯⎯⎯⎯⎯

21 ⎯⎯⎯⎯⎯⎯⎯⎯⎯⎯⎯⎯⎯⎯

19 ⎯⎯⎯⎯⎯⎯⎯⎯⎯⎯⎯⎯⎯⎯

22 ⎯⎯⎯⎯⎯⎯⎯⎯⎯⎯⎯⎯⎯⎯

Life is a splendid gift.
— Florence Nightingale

**Women Floating
Happily in the
Flow of Life**

July

23

26

24

27

25

28

July ★ August

29

30

31

1

2

3

August

4

5

6

7

8

9

August

10 ——————————

11 ——————————

12 ——————————

13 ——————————

14 ——————————

15 ——————————

There is time for work. And time for love. That leaves no other time.

— Coco Chanel

Every Mother Is a Hardworking Woman

August

16

19

17

20

18

21

August

22

25

23

26

24

27

August * September

28

31

29

1

30

2

September

3

4

5

6

7

8

September

9

10

11

12

13

14

September

15

16

17

18

19

20

First, no woman should say, "I am but a woman!" But a woman! What more could you ask to be?

— Maria Mitchell

Women Make the World Go 'Round

September

21

22

23

24

25

26

September ✶ October

27 ————————————————

30 ————————————————

28 ————————————————

1 ————————————————

29 ————————————————

2 ————————————————

October

3

6

4

7

5

8

October

9

10

11

12

13

14

Blessed is the
influence of one
true, loving human
soul on another.

— George Eliot
(Marian Evans)

Motherhood

63

October

15

18

16

19

17

20

October

21

22

23

24

25

26

October ✶ November

27

28

29

30

31

1

November

2

3

4

5

6

7

November

8

11

9

12

10

13

November

14

15

16

17

18

19

Woman must not accept; she must challenge . . . she must reverence that woman in her which struggles for expression.

– Margaret Sanger

Book-Woman

November

20

21

22

23

24

25

November * December

26

27

28

29

30

1

December

2

3

4

5

6

7

December

8

9

10

11

12

13

Guard within yourself
that treasure, kindness.

– George Sand
(Amandine Dupin)

Peace on Earth

75

December

14

15

16

17

18

19

December

20

21

22

23

24

25

December

26 ——————————————————

27 ——————————————————

28 ——————————————————

29 ——————————————————

30 ——————————————————

31 ——————————————————

Kiki Oberstenfeld de Suarez lives and paints in the beautiful highlands of Chiapas in southern Mexico. She is German by birth and upbringing, and a psychologist by education. More than ten years ago, chance brought her to the little colonial town of San Cristobal de las Casas, where she fell in love, started a family, and began to paint.

Kiki's paintings reflect the bold colors of the Mexican landscape and the vibrant culture of her adopted homeland. The images she chooses to paint express her belief in the good things of life – love, peace, friendship, fellowship, and a deep appreciation of nature and the wholeness of everything on earth. Her style is simple, honest, and personal, yet it is also universal, for it illustrates important values shared by people everywhere.

In just a few short years Kiki's fame has grown from a small Midwestern grass roots movement to worldwide recognition. Kiki is the author and illustrator of three children's books and her paintings, etchings, and licensed products are in great demand. Her artwork appears on posters, journals, greeting cards, T-shirts, nightshirts, sweatshirts, tote bags, and a myriad of associated products.

Photo © Larry LaBonté

Kiki

79

1994

JANUARY
```
 S  M  T  W  T  F  S
                   1
 2  3  4  5  6  7  8
 9 10 11 12 13 14 15
16 17 18 19 20 21 22
23 24 25 26 27 28 29
30 31
```

FEBRUARY
```
 S  M  T  W  T  F  S
       1  2  3  4  5
 6  7  8  9 10 11 12
13 14 15 16 17 18 19
20 21 22 23 24 25 26
27 28
```

MARCH
```
 S  M  T  W  T  F  S
       1  2  3  4  5
 6  7  8  9 10 11 12
13 14 15 16 17 18 19
20 21 22 23 24 25 26
27 28 29 30 31
```

APRIL
```
 S  M  T  W  T  F  S
                1  2
 3  4  5  6  7  8  9
10 11 12 13 14 15 16
17 18 19 20 21 22 23
24 25 26 27 28 29 30
```

MAY
```
 S  M  T  W  T  F  S
 1  2  3  4  5  6  7
 8  9 10 11 12 13 14
15 16 17 18 19 20 21
22 23 24 25 26 27 28
29 30 31
```

JUNE
```
 S  M  T  W  T  F  S
          1  2  3  4
 5  6  7  8  9 10 11
12 13 14 15 16 17 18
19 20 21 22 23 24 25
26 27 28 29 30
```

JULY
```
 S  M  T  W  T  F  S
                1  2
 3  4  5  6  7  8  9
10 11 12 13 14 15 16
17 18 19 20 21 22 23
24 25 26 27 28 29 30
31
```

AUGUST
```
 S  M  T  W  T  F  S
    1  2  3  4  5  6
 7  8  9 10 11 12 13
14 15 16 17 18 19 20
21 22 23 24 25 26 27
28 29 30 31
```

SEPTEMBER
```
 S  M  T  W  T  F  S
             1  2  3
 4  5  6  7  8  9 10
11 12 13 14 15 16 17
18 19 20 21 22 23 24
25 26 27 28 29 30
```

OCTOBER
```
 S  M  T  W  T  F  S
                   1
 2  3  4  5  6  7  8
 9 10 11 12 13 14 15
16 17 18 19 20 21 22
23 24 25 26 27 28 29
30 31
```

NOVEMBER
```
 S  M  T  W  T  F  S
       1  2  3  4  5
 6  7  8  9 10 11 12
13 14 15 16 17 18 19
20 21 22 23 24 25 26
27 28 29 30
```

DECEMBER
```
 S  M  T  W  T  F  S
             1  2  3
 4  5  6  7  8  9 10
11 12 13 14 15 16 17
18 19 20 21 22 23 24
25 26 27 28 29 30 31
```

1995

JANUARY
```
 S  M  T  W  T  F  S
 1  2  3  4  5  6  7
 8  9 10 11 12 13 14
15 16 17 18 19 20 21
22 23 24 25 26 27 28
29 30 31
```

FEBRUARY
```
 S  M  T  W  T  F  S
          1  2  3  4
 5  6  7  8  9 10 11
12 13 14 15 16 17 18
19 20 21 22 23 24 25
26 27 28
```

MARCH
```
 S  M  T  W  T  F  S
          1  2  3  4
 5  6  7  8  9 10 11
12 13 14 15 16 17 18
19 20 21 22 23 24 25
26 27 28 29 30 31
```

APRIL
```
 S  M  T  W  T  F  S
                   1
 2  3  4  5  6  7  8
 9 10 11 12 13 14 15
16 17 18 19 20 21 22
23 24 25 26 27 28 29
30
```

MAY
```
 S  M  T  W  T  F  S
    1  2  3  4  5  6
 7  8  9 10 11 12 13
14 15 16 17 18 19 20
21 22 23 24 25 26 27
28 29 30 31
```

JUNE
```
 S  M  T  W  T  F  S
             1  2  3
 4  5  6  7  8  9 10
11 12 13 14 15 16 17
18 19 20 21 22 23 24
25 26 27 28 29 30
```

JULY
```
 S  M  T  W  T  F  S
                   1
 2  3  4  5  6  7  8
 9 10 11 12 13 14 15
16 17 18 19 20 21 22
23 24 25 26 27 28 29
30 31
```

AUGUST
```
 S  M  T  W  T  F  S
       1  2  3  4  5
 6  7  8  9 10 11 12
13 14 15 16 17 18 19
20 21 22 23 24 25 26
27 28 29 30 31
```

SEPTEMBER
```
 S  M  T  W  T  F  S
                1  2
 3  4  5  6  7  8  9
10 11 12 13 14 15 16
17 18 19 20 21 22 23
24 25 26 27 28 29 30
```

OCTOBER
```
 S  M  T  W  T  F  S
 1  2  3  4  5  6  7
 8  9 10 11 12 13 14
15 16 17 18 19 20 21
22 23 24 25 26 27 28
29 30 31
```

NOVEMBER
```
 S  M  T  W  T  F  S
          1  2  3  4
 5  6  7  8  9 10 11
12 13 14 15 16 17 18
19 20 21 22 23 24 25
26 27 28 29 30
```

DECEMBER
```
 S  M  T  W  T  F  S
                1  2
 3  4  5  6  7  8  9
10 11 12 13 14 15 16
17 18 19 20 21 22 23
24 25 26 27 28 29 30
31
```

1996

JANUARY
```
 S  M  T  W  T  F  S
    1  2  3  4  5  6
 7  8  9 10 11 12 13
14 15 16 17 18 19 20
21 22 23 24 25 26 27
28 29 30 31
```

FEBRUARY
```
 S  M  T  W  T  F  S
             1  2  3
 4  5  6  7  8  9 10
11 12 13 14 15 16 17
18 19 20 21 22 23 24
25 26 27 28 29
```

MARCH
```
 S  M  T  W  T  F  S
                1  2
 3  4  5  6  7  8  9
10 11 12 13 14 15 16
17 18 19 20 21 22 23
24 25 26 27 28 29 30
31
```

APRIL
```
 S  M  T  W  T  F  S
    1  2  3  4  5  6
 7  8  9 10 11 12 13
14 15 16 17 18 19 20
21 22 23 24 25 26 27
28 29 30
```

MAY
```
 S  M  T  W  T  F  S
          1  2  3  4
 5  6  7  8  9 10 11
12 13 14 15 16 17 18
19 20 21 22 23 24 25
26 27 28 29 30 31
```

JUNE
```
 S  M  T  W  T  F  S
                   1
 2  3  4  5  6  7  8
 9 10 11 12 13 14 15
16 17 18 19 20 21 22
23 24 25 26 27 28 29
30
```

JULY
```
 S  M  T  W  T  F  S
    1  2  3  4  5  6
 7  8  9 10 11 12 13
14 15 16 17 18 19 20
21 22 23 24 25 26 27
28 29 30 31
```

AUGUST
```
 S  M  T  W  T  F  S
             1  2  3
 4  5  6  7  8  9 10
11 12 13 14 15 16 17
18 19 20 21 22 23 24
25 26 27 28 29 30 31
```

SEPTEMBER
```
 S  M  T  W  T  F  S
 1  2  3  4  5  6  7
 8  9 10 11 12 13 14
15 16 17 18 19 20 21
22 23 24 25 26 27 28
29 30
```

OCTOBER
```
 S  M  T  W  T  F  S
       1  2  3  4  5
 6  7  8  9 10 11 12
13 14 15 16 17 18 19
20 21 22 23 24 25 26
27 28 29 30 31
```

NOVEMBER
```
 S  M  T  W  T  F  S
                1  2
 3  4  5  6  7  8  9
10 11 12 13 14 15 16
17 18 19 20 21 22 23
24 25 26 27 28 29 30
```

DECEMBER
```
 S  M  T  W  T  F  S
 1  2  3  4  5  6  7
 8  9 10 11 12 13 14
15 16 17 18 19 20 21
22 23 24 25 26 27 28
29 30 31
```

1997

JANUARY
```
 S  M  T  W  T  F  S
          1  2  3  4
 5  6  7  8  9 10 11
12 13 14 15 16 17 18
19 20 21 22 23 24 25
26 27 28 29 30 31
```

FEBRUARY
```
 S  M  T  W  T  F  S
                   1
 2  3  4  5  6  7  8
 9 10 11 12 13 14 15
16 17 18 19 20 21 22
23 24 25 26 27 28
```

MARCH
```
 S  M  T  W  T  F  S
                   1
 2  3  4  5  6  7  8
 9 10 11 12 13 14 15
16 17 18 19 20 21 22
23 24 25 26 27 28 29
30 31
```

APRIL
```
 S  M  T  W  T  F  S
       1  2  3  4  5
 6  7  8  9 10 11 12
13 14 15 16 17 18 19
20 21 22 23 24 25 26
27 28 29 30
```

MAY
```
 S  M  T  W  T  F  S
          1  2  3
 4  5  6  7  8  9 10
11 12 13 14 15 16 17
18 19 20 21 22 23 24
25 26 27 28 29 30 31
```

JUNE
```
 S  M  T  W  T  F  S
 1  2  3  4  5  6  7
 8  9 10 11 12 13 14
15 16 17 18 19 20 21
22 23 24 25 26 27 28
29 30
```

JULY
```
 S  M  T  W  T  F  S
       1  2  3  4  5
 6  7  8  9 10 11 12
13 14 15 16 17 18 19
20 21 22 23 24 25 26
27 28 29 30 31
```

AUGUST
```
 S  M  T  W  T  F  S
                1  2
 3  4  5  6  7  8  9
10 11 12 13 14 15 16
17 18 19 20 21 22 23
24 25 26 27 28 29 30
31
```

SEPTEMBER
```
 S  M  T  W  T  F  S
    1  2  3  4  5  6
 7  8  9 10 11 12 13
14 15 16 17 18 19 20
21 22 23 24 25 26 27
28 29 30
```

OCTOBER
```
 S  M  T  W  T  F  S
          1  2  3  4
 5  6  7  8  9 10 11
12 13 14 15 16 17 18
19 20 21 22 23 24 25
26 27 28 29 30 31
```

NOVEMBER
```
 S  M  T  W  T  F  S
                   1
 2  3  4  5  6  7  8
 9 10 11 12 13 14 15
16 17 18 19 20 21 22
23 24 25 26 27 28 29
30
```

DECEMBER
```
 S  M  T  W  T  F  S
    1  2  3  4  5  6
 7  8  9 10 11 12 13
14 15 16 17 18 19 20
21 22 23 24 25 26 27
28 29 30 31
```